Poems, Prose and Phases

This is a decade of creative works about my journey and the different phases in my life. My poetry, my attempt at short stories and musical lyrics all compiled. All works are either about thoughts, ideas, perspectives or actual situations, personal and non-personal that have occurred. All of the things that I have witnessed experienced, and that just wandered in my mind. This is dedicated to a decade of growth, challenge and change. I have come this far and I continue to move forward. Welcome to the phases of my life.

Edited by Raquel Penzo

ISBN 978-0-557-99499-1

Question 13

I handed in my application.
"Question 13 is incorrect" she said,
So, I checked, but it wasn't,
It stated: Are you an American citizen?
Could I blame her?
I'm five feet tall with
Long midnight hair and dark eyes
She must have thought I was a:
Bean-frying,
Burrito-making,
Taco-selling,
Tamale-eating,
Poncho-wearing,
Person.
Okay,
But, I am an American too.

America's Divine Image

Cruelty is a woman's mink coat
Abuse has the hands of a rapist
Lies have the tongue of a counterfeit prophet
Loneliness is a homeless man surrounded by pigeons
Hate is the face of a dictator
Ego enjoys clothing stores with mirrors
Lust is a billionaire beseeching for more money
Pity is having to vote between two bad choices

Across the painting

He sits in his grandmother's rocking chair,
writing with his left hand, unnaturally,
sitting across a painting of
arms wrestling between the smoke,
bruised hands, bloody hands,
hands that worked all day hands,
hands in fists, fighting through the smog.

Inside a building, with right hands stretched out,
are many men in the big black boots and hats,
holding big black books,
crowds in rows wait for them,
tired mothers and children, hopeless seniors,
the sick and handicapped hidden inside the dark.
A curious child peeks through a broken window.

Millions of six pointed stars bundled and burned,
Torah pages and prayer shawls buried six feet,
strings of curls lying in a corner,
fathers and husbands outside in lines, duct-taped
mouths,
while waiting for a signal, staring into the heavens,
their eyes look up and meet with the little boy outside
the painting, sitting in his grandmother's rocking chair.

P.I.G. (Prisoner in Germany)

"Strip, you pig," says the officer to the man,
The man obeys and lies on the hot ground,

a frying pan.
The man becomes sweaty, oily and toasty,
then shrivels up.
Flesh rags, like slices, hang from his corpse.

Here Is Where She Sits

There is a field of grass and weeds,
Across from it an ocean,
Above it a boardwalk,
Here is where she sits.

Her feet dangle in the air,
As she stares at the sky,
Shades of pink, blue and purple,
For once she is at peace.

But she knows she will end up back in her bed,
Her house,
A so-called hell,
A puzzle,
A maze,
Life.

Wasted Time

She spends on beauty products,
ageless skin creams,
hair dyes,
body waxing,body masking,
pedicures and manicures,
the cure for her age.

She sets her watch half an hour early,
a vegetarian,
exercising daily,
looks 40,
thinks 30,
acts 20,
every year on the beach,
bronzing.
She sobs and sighs
attempting to appear ageless,
but it fails to every
second beneath
the sun.

The DNA of a Liar

Too many sell their souls,
Settle for less and regress,
I'm not impressed with their paper,
From getting blows to the chest,
Swollen knees for a price,
And left alone to regret,
Swimming in paper could never ever help you forget,
Quickly switching positions,
Shady snitching for riches,
Appearance may be appealing,
But rotten souls go to ditches,
The DNA of a liar,
Will sell you out for a dollar,
With Judas kisses and handshakes,
The plots and schemes of a scholar.

The Serpent Man

His
toxic
scaled lips
spat
out acid
every time
he spoke,
it burned
my skin.
Toasted,
wrinkled,
discolored,
I tried to
peel off
his residue,
the sting was
unbearable.
And what
hurt most were
the words
that swam
within the
venom,
implanted
into
me…

Queens in August

A broken boardwalk, dark sand,
empty seashells, shattered glass,
dead horseshoe crabs,
sand fleas, candy wrappers,
murky water, a one-eyed pigeon,
no-lifeguard-on-duty signs,
tons of seaweed, charcoal, a dead June bug,
burnt bamboo paper laying on a rock,
empty glass coke bottles filled with sand,
a stray dog doing his duties,
a broken fishing rod, dead fish,
a wrinkled beach ball,
an armless Barbie,
a child's handprints in the sand,
a sand castle.

The Rainbow Tree

My daddy sat on his high horse,
And for the first time, he brought me to the fields.
I remember seeing a rainbow,
One unlike any other,
And he pointed to the meadows,
And he pointed to the trees.
He promised me new colors that I have never seen.
The sky wasn't cloudy,
Just a big blue canvas,
The grass shone like wet emeralds,
The rich soil was maroon,
And a tall tree stood in the middle.

He touched the tree and swung the big loop hanging from it. He sang:
"Blue Black, Brown, Red bone and High Yellow all gone
"Blue Black, Brown, Red bone and High Yellow gonna find me one tomorrow."
Those colors were the part rainbow that was on the ground,
And its pain was red and rooted into the bumpy soil.
The bloody loop is still there.
No longer just any loop to me.
I moved to the city, but sometimes visit the rainbow tree.
I hear it cry often,
My father lies beneath the soil in torment.

Half to Hate

Between two religions,
Two different nations,
I am good and evil,
So I believe,
50% of my blood is infected.
What were my parents thinking?
Peel off my flesh,
Well, at least half,
But, I have a plan!
My pain will heal others,
Half breeds like me.
As I raise my right arm forward,
And brush my mustache neat,
I say:
A pure nation must come forth,
And more than six million will suffer for my-self hated.

B*TCH

B.I.T.C.H. now that's a word that I hate,
It puts me in a negative state,
It's a negative trait,
A dog and I could never relate,
My rate is like gold,
I'm valuable and G-d broke the mold.
You must have it backwards,
The D.O.G. you see is really the G.-.D.
Made in the image of beauty, I'm gorgeous, you see.
Don't try to put me down because I'll go to the top,
Rise above, stretch and reach,
I'm the cream of the crop.
Never stop, I'll refuse to be seen on a leash,
Verbal abuse? Are you hating on me?

B is for Beautiful
I is for Intelligent
T is for my Temple and you know I had to mention it,
C is for Creating words more valuable than gold and gems,
H is for my presence, in High-definition.

And just to mention,
The next time you say that word to me,
Those five little letters I take very personally,
Just tell your mother, then your sister and your daughter to listen to a man disrespecting generations of women.

A Frown

food control,
weight-loss pills,
one-year membership to a gym,
oversized shirt,
sweat pants,
exercise bikes,
fitness instructor in your face,
an iPod,
bottles of water,
calorie counting,
low-carb intakes,
jogging with a friend,
salads for lunch,
measuring tape,
a scale,
smaller jeans,
a pat on the back,
walk to work,
a sudden crush on a co-worker,
protein bars,
gallons of water
spandex pants,
sports bra,
light weightlifting,
a belt,
new shoes,
a baby blue tee,
little black dress from high school,
an office party,
your crush on a date with someone else,
a strong drink,

sitting alone,
a cab ride home,
watching television,
cheating on vanilla bean ice-cream,
A frown.

Eyes Pass the Hour

The rusted swings rocked
As the breeze yawned,
The sun became cold and pallid.
A brown paper kite tangled itself
In the branches where yellow eyes
Peeked from inside a tree.
She lay her silver head on the russet grass,
And waited for the stars to vanish.
She stared at the uneven yellow eyes
Until they closed.
The last scarlet leaf fell off the tree.
The eyes became hands,
The hands were the time,
The last tick,
The last beat,
Her last breath.

Flowerpots

A mother had three flowerpots,
She obsessed for them daily,
One day she watered them too much.
The Lily's stem was bent,

The Marigold had drowned,
The Violet's petals were crushed.
The mother ran and told her three daughters,
"Why are my plants are dying? I am always attending them."
Her daughters shook their heads and said together:
"Now do you understand how we feel?"

A Vision

of sitting on porcupine quills,
maroon lakes rising at her feet,
soaring, swollen eyes
created high hills of liquid salt,
from a man's
constant nagging,
demands,
and complaints.
Waiting to see
how long it would last,
until he would cool off again.
Building the courage,
the strength to
finally remove those quills
from where she sits.

The Garden

I planted a seed without a name
And watched it grow.
The seed became a sprout,

The sprout became a bud,
The bud was unrecognizable.
Its stem was bent.
My mother's flowers bloomed beautifully.
Did I not do exactly what my mother did?
What was so different?
She smiled when she planted,
When I planted, I was sad.
I planted a seed to that failed to blossom,
And I watched it wither away.

The FRAUD

I refuse to saturate the words,
Logics,
Books,
Opinions
Theories,
Beliefs,
Of a tainted, angry atheist, antisocial, cocaine addict.
A FRAUD,
And his name
Is only
A vowel away to
Prove it.

Tracings of Chalk

If it wasn't for the L-rd,
I would be in a tracing of chalk,
But He told me to knock,

I called on His name,
The doors unlocked,
And I was saved,
No longer enslaved,
He set this captive free,
But now I have to behave.

The Sour Hour

Ready for battle,
Here comes a war,
Bring the:
Cults, trends and fakes down,
In the name of the L-rd.
It's the breaking down of doors,
the devil has been exposed,
Strip!
Fall to your knees and
now put on some clothes.
Lives being victimized
the killing of sheep,
the enemies waiting patiently
together they reap.
I saw the game,
lying for the money and fame,
friends are now my enemies
but victory I gain.
They hide behind smiles,
the hugs gave me denials,
conversations meaningless,
artificial and foul.

But I smelled it,
Wild lifestyles
Dry and mild,
Lukewarm soldiers only last for a while,
The mission is to spread
common sense and the truth,
like a virus overrunning
to the old and to the youth,
Conviction scares and scatters to the soul's
points of views,
if you get offended
then these messages are for you.

Souls on Sale

To all my people on the wrong route,
Females passing draws out,
Fellas getting smoked out,
Children dying? No doubt,
Now cut it out!
Now, what's that all about?
Your lives have been planned out,
but still ya wanna bug out?
You live without love,
You live without hope,
Hanging with the wrong crowd
then you looking to get smoked, It's not a joke.
(Not here to provoke you, just here to help you...I care about you.)

Too young to be in the streets
jumping from sheets to sheets

Smoking and robbing
Destruction of innocent sheep.
Drinking and driving,
Not living but dying,
Trying to be an example
cause talk is cheap.
Killing each other for a medallion
Mothers going all out crying
Fatherless babies
They need to set their eyes on Zion.
Don't be standing still
Plan ahead or plan to fail
The future isn't sweet,
when your souls are on sale.

Soles of Souls

The soles of souls stomp and stampede, searching for salvation. Seeking sentiments within strangers and scanning speculations for solutions. It's a sad secluded world although you are never in solitude, surrounded by societies whose motives are suspect and selfish; I sympathize for my lost species, unaware of their significance, misguided by the shade and shadows of sinful spirits, instead of striding toward light as the salt of the earth. But I remain optimistic and I hope these seeds become steams and sprout by the Holy Superior's rain, may it create a spark that will emerge into an inner flame.

The Sad Little Note

Once upon a time,
There was a conductor and his musical staff.
He had a treble clef and a time signature and
Many notes on a path of the staff.

But there was one little note,
That wanted to shift his position.
To be ahead of the other notes,
To be in the spotlight to glistened,

The conductor allowed him,
To do what he pleased.
The little note rearranged all the notes
And even changed the reprise.

Once the show went on,
The song was no longer the same.
All because of one little note,
The conductor failed to tame.

Tap,
    Tap,
        Tap,
            Tap

The little note worked twice as hard,
Goodbye half-note,
Pushed himself even further,

Removing the whole note too,
He replaced the sixteenth
And also the eight,
The little note wanted all the attention,
He felt that he was great.

Then the conductor took a look
At his musical staff,
The little note was all alone,
The little note started to laugh.

The conducted sat in regret,
And accepted his mistake,
To allow one little note
To destroy what took so long to create.

TEAM

There was once a **TEAM** that was so strong in accord, until the letter **I** came along and made the team work backwards. Little by little the team fell apart. The letter **I** then threw the **TEAM** into the trash like old **MEAT.** The letter **I** stood alone.

The Rapper was Unwrapped

He was a rapper,
But not successful in the world,
The industry never gave him a break,
His plan began to unfurl,
So he tried another route,
Needed to accomplish his dream,
He was a go-getter,
With his words, he fooled many,
Was a light among the strangers?
Provided darkness to his brothers,
When he spoke he said one thing,
And when he walked did another.
But the rapper was unwrapped,
And many saw his false motives,
Whatever he touched,
Successful in the outside
But his heart was corrosive,
You can't get crunked in the church!
A religious gangsta and no heist?
Bunch of babble and foolishness,
Creating gang signs for Christ? What?
Instead of listening he's talking,
Instead of slowing down he speeds.
Put the mic down for a minute,
And pick up your Torah and read.

A Mic Check

A mic check,
Eleven is on the set,
On the mic I come correct,
There's no beef,
Just mad respect,
There's no stress when I express,
About My L-rd, because I'm blessed,
Even though I'm put through many tests,
The outcome is success.

Frozen

The thorn on a rose made her
Suck
Taste
An accidental cut.
Bitter and
Cold,
As she pressed her finger.

A drop of blood falls on the concrete.
From red to
Transparent,
Icy and frigid,
She took a napkin to wipe it,
But it tore.

A homeless man is sitting by a
Grocery store,
Observant,
Noticing,
And shouted
"Incubate your heart!"

She gawked and
Remained puzzled,
Rolled her eyes and walked away.
"Mad old man," she whispered.
But afterwards,

She felt convicted,
Turned around to questioned him,
But he was gone.

Just a feather lay on the ground.

Miles Davis' Face on the Tutu Album

A black sky
two blue crescent moons reflected
inside two dark suns,
below it
a mountain
sitting above
two steep hills
and a valley

separating a
waterfall and
cool breeze.
Inside,
thousands of boxed ivory
tightening
onyx and gold
an umbilical cord
attached
to jazz.

Inhale…

Natural spring water
with a smear of
sweet honey,
milk,
pink satin peony petals,
scent of the earth,
essence of the rain.
Now
sleep,
sweat,
saturate and lather,
over your smooth skin,
cool blue, and pink
bubbles.
It's a spray mist.

Mercy, Mercy, Mercy (Poem for Cannonball Adderly)

Is that church folk music?
That sax plays like sin,
Mercy, mercy, mercy.
Thrill
Tempt
Taunt
Tease
That sax sure can please,
Mercy, mercy, mercy.
Forgive
Forget
Repent
Repeat
L-rd, is that church folk music?
I am far from my knees,
Mercy, mercy, mercy.

Before Creation*(Inspired by William Blake's* The Tyger*)*

So they say He is a spirit,
All powerful,
I believe.
That He is all good,
And gave free will,
I agree.
He created the Lamb,
Did He create the snake, too?
Or was the snake once fangless?
Like a harmless worm,

That turned into a venomous viper.

Whom Do You Worship?

Do you worship your pastor?

Or do you serve the Messiah,

Yeshua, the true master?

Things Are Critical

Things are critical,
A low bar in the spiritual,
Religious and political,
Fast money and hypocritical.
Artificial, superficial, fanged wolves in fleece,
Hand dipped in the grease,
Foul scent when they speak.
Because
When you sin with your mind
then you sin in your heart,

When you sin in the physical,
you sin when you walk,

When you sin in the spiritual
you sin when you talk,

All sin is critical just give him your heart
Cotton hands walk around and bald sheep lying in chalk.

Who works in factories disguised as sanctuaries?
Con artists pushing boundaries,
Doing blasphemies,
No different from the ones who sit in D.C.
Creating lies of false hope and deceit.
Burning facts, creating myths
And then spread them like seeds.

People Are Just People

I've been dissed by my brethren,
And praised by the heathen,
I can't believe that I'm dreaming
When I am wide awake,
Are the congregations at stake?
When the world gives you love,
But the brethren show hate?
People are just people,
Don't rely on them,
The church is a clinic,
And we are all sick,
The L-rd is showing us
To only rely on HIM.

No Affection, No Desire

No affection, no desire,
I am cold as a rock,
Better yet like diamonds,
They don't mean much.
Not like the sunset on the beach,
Not like a milky sky in the winter,
Just cold and numb.

Sold for Less than Gold

...He is are the L, lacking in the word Gold
More powerful than any currency,
Similar to the element in which His Son was sold.

The Heart

As the heart fails to swell,
Fails to get well but repel,
It tries to heal once again,
It's on life support receiving messages
From the brain
Saying: "Your heart is in pain."
But you know what they say,
If you love it, let it go,
If it comes back it's yours,
If not,
It never was.

You Are My First
You are my first,
My one and only,
The one who always keeps it holy,
The only that never kept me lonely,
L-rd, you're never phony.
Listen, you taught me the truth,
Now what should I do?
Speak it, and I'm making that move.

Love from Up Above

Lyrics of love to all those who are:
Needing a hug,
Dealing with drugs,
Dealing with thugs,
Dancing in clubs,
Living for bucks,
Sipping some bub,
Sleeping with bugs,
Looking to snug up with life-sized slugs,
Lifelines slow, hanging onto a plug,
Once you let go,
You're six feet below the green rug,
But real love is only found when looking up above.
Just look up.

Walking the Walk

I feel like I'm walking on a very thin thread,
And if I fall, below is a six foot bed,
The narrow path,
Please L-rd; guide me on this road,
Without you, I won't make it on this thin dental floss.

Live, Laugh, Listen, Learn, Labor, Love, Life. (Phrases for Phases)

I will sing to the L-rd all my life; I will sing praise to my G-d as long as I **Live**. *Psalm 104:33*

Our mouths were filled with **Laugh**ter, our tongues with songs of joy. *Psalm 126:2*

Joshua said to the Israelites, "Come here and **Listen** to the words of the L-rd your G-d. *Joshua 3:9*

I will praise you with an upright heart as I **Learn** your righteous laws. *Psalm 119:7*

Everyone should be quick to **Listen**, slow to speak and slow to become angry. *James 1:19*

You will eat the fruit of your **Labor**; blessings and prosperity will be yours. *Psalm 128:2*

Mercy, peace and **Love** be yours in abundance. *Jude 1:2*

Hold on to instruction; do not let it go; guard it well, for it is your **Life**. *Proverbs 4:13*

The Terrible Tree

He was eleven years old,
In the fifth grade and with a mouth like a sailor,
He spent his afternoons in detention and received daily phone calls home.
One day the teacher had enough. She brought him to the new school psychologist. It was the school psychologist's first day. Her office was small, plain and had a fresh scent of warm vanilla sugar.
The boy went into her office and sat down in her chair with his hands folded, as if there were a halo above his head.
The school psychologist handed him blue pen and paper.
"Seth, please sit."
Seth obeyed.
"Here take this, and please write down everything you are feeling," she said as she studied him.
He wrote, doodled, and sketched.
Words of anger, meanness, and sadness.
When he was done he gave her the paper.
"Do you see this page Seth? May all these negative thoughts and feelings disappear?"
She ripped the paper and threw it in the trash.
Seth shrugged his shoulders and laughed and said

"Those words may be in the trash now, but I still have them in my mind." She looked up at the clock. It was now 3:15. They exited the office. All the lights were off and the school was empty. Only a custodian cleaning was left behind. He cleaned all the classrooms and threw out the trash. Seth's torn up paper was at the top of the pile.

As the custodian took the untied garbage bag outside, a light breeze blew the torn papers into the wind and unto the grass of the schoolyard. It began to rain. The soil saturated the paper.

Weeks passed and the green grass grew. A baby tree came forth. The tree's bark was dark blue, its leaves were white with blue stripes, and the fruit it produced looked like tiny alphabet letters and were poisonous. As the tree grew, it caused injury. The branches whacked the pedestrians as they walked by. The trunk had sharp and pointy thorns and had a foul stench of mildew and mold. The town became upset. Many members of the community questioned the existence of the tree and wanted it gone.

The principal of the school asked to city council to remove the tree. But the tree was strong and rooted to the ground. Everyone noticed how the lumbermen struggled to remove the tree. The neighbors of the town all brought their axes and tried to cut it down themselves, but that was unsuccessful. The axes all broke. Everyone ran mad looking for safety away from the tree.

Seth examined the tree and walked toward it.

"Hey kid, get out of there," said one of the community members. But Seth continued to walk toward it.

He picked up a fruit without fear. The fruit did not harm him like it had harmed everyone else. As he looked closer at the fruit he noticed the tiny letters began to form words. Each fruit asked a question. *What is the antonym of Hate?* Seth scratched his head and wished he would have paid attention in his English class. He took a guess and said bad. The fruit shocked him. The fruit fell on the ground and bounced back into his hand. *Try again it stated.* Seth tried again.

"Antonym of hate? Is that an opposite? Is it love?"

The fruit spelled out **L-O-V-E** and the leaves of the tree fell to the ground. Seth picked up another fruit. *What is a three letter word for happy?*

"Joy!" shouted Seth with excitement

The fruit spelled out **J-O-Y**, and the awful tree stench was gone. Seth continued to read out the answers as the tree slowly began to diminish. **P-E-A-C-E** the thorns became dull. **K-I-N-.D-N-E-S-S**, **G-E-N-T-L-E-N-E-S-S, G-O-O-D-N-E...**but before Seth could finish the rest of the questions, the ground began to shake. The roots of the tree were loosened.

Seth ran away from the tree as it began to tilt over. It fell on the ground. Blue maggots wiggled at the end of its roots. The maggots formed words like: hate, anger, and fear. They stopped wiggling and turn into dust. The tree dried up. Seth stood in amazement as the town began to cheer him on. They carried him for his victory. The principal smiled at him and cheered him on as well. Seth looked around to see if he could find the school psychologist but he could not. As the town continued to cheer, he ran into the school to tell the school psychologist what happened. But when Seth got there her office was gone. It was a dark and empty janitor's closet with only a pile of feathers on the ground.

The Technicolor Illusion

Through her eyes, and only ten years old,
She tries to comprehend the facts and the fabrication.
In a world of opposites, with elders who try to correct.
But she, along with others, reject the information.
"They" don't understand her dialects.
Where mathematics is outside in the corner,
Those who seek otherwise are loners,
She chooses fantasy, but not in dolls and tales,
But in magazines, music, and press-on nails.
"What do I want to be when I grow up?
A money-maker, a soul-shaker,
An eye-pleaser, and flesh-teaser.
Poor little lost lass,
Looking at the world through Technicolor glass,
Along with her there are a mass
Of other little girls with the same illusion.

A Movie Set Called Life

Life is like a movie,
I lived through so many episodes,
Some were was cut and unused,
But others successful,

And in the moment,
I did not comprehend,
The things that were not for me,
And now I sit on the passenger side,
And now HE is the one steering,

L-rd, I apologize, I did not understand at the time,
All the times you protected me from all of the grim,
What seems right, really isn't
And I'm glad you protected me,
And so I thank you for not letting me complete the rest of the scenes.

From Amen to Amen

When I was young,
I asked my grandmother a question about my faith.
She shushed me,
Shooed me and
Slapped me across the face.

"You should never question G-d, it is never okay,
Just believe what I tell you. And you will be saved."
I just wanted a solution to my confusion.

I was young and foolish and not guided by truth.

If a man is singular
And men are plural
What was 'Amen'?
Was it blasphemous to ask?

I just held on to my bible,
But never opened it at all,
Never questioned again,
I just did what I saw.

I wanted to please the L-rd,
And so I did what I learned,
Was I meant to see shadows?
So a ministry I had earned.

I continued to hop over incense,
Place quarters in rice,
Place garlic heads in my pocket.
Listen to Walter Mercado's advice.

Decorated the idols,
Placed alconfor in back of the doors,
Tied loose hairs into knots,
Held sacred the talisman that I wore.

Face readings and palm readings,
Underwear worn inside out,
Guided by astrology and numerology,

Was this what G-d was about?

Innocent and ignorant,
Until I picked up that book,
But this time I read it,
The pages flipped and they took

Me to Deuteronomy,
Conviction and correction,
And now nothing has been the same,
My vision is now different,
And now I am aware of the enemy's game.
Amen to the truth,
So be it, in you, too!

The Smile

You tell me to smile,
But I am smiling.
My smile doesn't look like yours.
Yours is upside down.
When I am smiling,
You ask me, "Why am I smiling?"
I tell you that I am not,
My cheekbones are just real high.
My smiles are just a
Meaningless mass of muscles moving up and down,
Yet, they affect lives.

The Pressure of a Diamond

Tested by the fire, and surrounded by heat,
pure diamonds manifest, no time to retreat.
It's hard for a soldier, alone like a straw,
but the glory belongs to G-d,
and so do all of my wars.
I pray that the angels guide me
and stay beside me when I am weak,
that they protect me and my family and all of my peeps.
This path is real narrow, walking on dental floss,
asking G-d why me?
Trying to figure my flaws.
Trying to seek all my errors,
instead of counting my blessings,
I'm only human and wrestling with this flesh that's
battling.
But the glory belongs to G-d,
and so do my wars.

Revolution

We need a revolution,
A resolution
Avoid the confusion,
And seek a conclusion,
G-d is our only is the Solution,

So in G-d we trust,
And it's a must,
That we expose America's lust.

Latinos Unidos

We've been raped, slaughtered and slaved,
Given government names,
We walk with heads low
Because we stay feeling ashamed,
But my people once reigned,
Now catch them in bodegas,
Incas, Mayans, Aztecas, and Tainos selling manteca!
Instead of staying in la escuela,
They stay watching novellas,
Illusions and delusions.
My people wake up!
It's time for restitution!

Mira Esa

Mira esa,
Do you see her?
She is at the lake staring at her reflection,
Only five feet tall yet still part of a nation,
Inside of her are genes of a great civilization.
You call her a wet-back?

But you stand on her land.
Who do think named Texas, Nevada, Florida, California,
Las Vegas and Colorado man?

Venting at Veracity *(Lyrics)*

Generations have gone mad,
Myspace teens now hold future interns
For porn mags, now what a drag.
A free show for alter egos
and employers now know,
Who is getting hired and who has to go (You're fired).
Chivalry is so dead,
Subway carts full of women standing,
While the men sit and stare.
Senior citizens once respected, we need their for advice,
But the youth believes they have all the answers,
And they call themselves wise.
Life is so backwards
It's hard to reach to the top,
Friends and foes look the same,
Hard to know who is genuine and who is not.
People love to praise all those who come out of jail,
But hate on the ones who graduate and try to prevail,
The mentality of keeping it real
While living in the slums,
No wonder the government has every reason to believe
that we are dumb.

A Rose without a Stem

Trapped in this world,
A rose without a stem,
Who are you fooling girl?
Not me, but maybe them.

Trapped in this world,
A rose without a steam,
Like Ms. Hill said
Don't be a hard rock when you really are a gem.

Hard Rock or Gem

I know your kind,
You're a leader,
Yeah you got your own mind,
A little thug,
Pretty rough,
But your heart is alright.
A hard rock?
Who are you fooling girl?
You are really a jewel,
And when someone gets too close,
For your protection you're rude.
You watch your back often,
Keep your eyes open,

Guard your grill,
Focus your mind,
Without a word spoken,
Write what's in your heart,
But say what's in your head,
Pray to G-d every night,
But still wish you were dead.
Your grades aren't too good,
You have low self-esteem,
Suffer from social anxiety,
Yeah, I know what you mean.
Because where you're at, I was,
And were you've been I already left.
So use my experience to guide your steps.

Been There, Done That

I've been there, and done that,
I know the aftermath,
When you were going,
I was coming back,
Walking the same path,
I tried to do the math,
Doing what I wanted to,
Living my life without a clue,
Living in sin by multitudes.
Walking on deep slopes,
Sidewalks just like tight ropes,
Chocking on venom

From all the evil I spoke.
I did not know any better,
Releasing stress through letters,
Choked up and heated,
Life in a turtleneck sweater,
Could this get better?
I don't want it to get worse.
Wondering all these years if my life was cursed.
Wanted to burst out,
Yell and scream for help.
On a flight triple six, I was going to hell.
But things got well
And I excelled,
Now I stay analyzing Isaiah Chapter 12.
Whatever didn't make it into your future,
Then it's time to move on,
Better blessings out there,
So seek them, before they're gone.

***Mi Dios Es** *(Lyrics to Ride Wit Me)*

Mi dios es hermoso, no fantasioso,
Te digo porque es la verdad.
Es real lo que te digo,
Su palabra es cumplido,
Nunca está suspendido,
Pues lo puedo escuchar.
Lo siento en el templo,
Y lo siento en mi pecho,

Corazón está contento,
Yo ya quero llorar.
Su nombre hace Guerra,
Dile a cualquera,
Venimos en el nombre de dios para la tierra.

G-d Is Good

My G-d is gracious,
His words are outrageous,
His love contagious,
His love amazes.
Spread His love to all the nations,
Because I am courageous,
But only through Him,
Like kryptonite is to Superman,
My weakness is sin.
Avoid the negativity,
Temptation is near,
Stay focused when I'm talking because the devil can hear.
The world is detrimental,
Superficial and judgmental,
Artificial monumental,
Temporary and just a rental.
But G-d is beneficial,
And Yeshua died for your sins,
We are here for a purpose,
To begin once again, be born again,

To repent, but not repeat.
With G-d in my life,
My life is so complete.

Predicaments

The veterans still sleep inside the trains.
Loose harlots, $5 for brains,
And the biggest pimps are still leading assembly.
Church is mundane,
And all is obtained,
For a tax refund and a quick name change (pastor).
Little girls who used to jump roped in the streets,
Now wear opposite colors,
Stay looking for beef.
The baby boy who once crawled in his crib,
Grew up, got shot,
Blasted his legs and tore open his ribs.
Peeping Tom lives next to your house,
Friendly text messages to go up in your blouse,
Now he and his spouse,
Are unemployed and stay on the web,
Videotaping what goes in their bed.
Fast money instead,
Sexy mamis showing all of their flesh,
I.D. card stating they're not even 18 yet,
No bosom or chest.
And there are real dudes, who work hard,
But are dedicated tippers,

Trying to wife up local strippers?
No money, yet the world goes 'round,
Predicaments we all go through to take off a frown.

Predicaments II

Verse two,
Still nothing new,
Hustlers still hustling,
They gotta do what they do,
Gotta do what you know,
Gotta do what you see,
Monkey see, monkey do always gets you to eat.
Cause we are never awake,
It's the government way,
We try to survive,
But the enemy waits.
And things must change.
When baby mamas got cases,
No longer working,
Child support replacing minimum wages.
Now I'm making tuna fish and rice for dinner again,
Eviction notices and credit card debt,
Prevent me from spending.
When jobs are lost,
The hours get cut,
Rent goes up,
There is never enough,
Can't even find a part time,

With a college degree,
Up in my neck indeed.
Life is a test,
And I've run out of breath.

The Project's Anthem

This is our national anthem,
To those who think we are phantoms,
But we are here and we're voiceless,
And continue throwing tantrums.

It's the anthem of the hopeless,
But never letting go of our pride,
Against the N.W.O and the rest of the lies.

The anthem against injustice,
Of the crooked cops that drive by,
The years of court dates that prevents us to strive.

The anthem to remain hopeful,
But hungry and unemployed,
Our heads remain held high although feelings destroyed.

The anthem of our prayers,
And our eyes focus to the sky,
Although we are poor, our eyes are on the prize.

The Wormy Apple

The apple is bittersweet
When you are walking these streets,
From BX, Brooklyn, Harlem, Staten Island and Queens,
I've been to many beautiful places,
But I can't manage to leave,
There is something about NYC,
I keep turning my cheek.

The City Named Twice

If I ever leave,
Will I…
Miss the grey skies,
And grey subway cats,
The miniature, pregnant dinosaurs in my kitchen,
The six-plus floors without elevators,
The two-year rent increases,
And pay cuts and hour decreases.
My B.A. is rubbish?
And the view outside my window is no different,
The barrios and the ghettos,
Projects and experiments,
The protection of auxiliary police,
Crowded Dunkin Donuts with NYPD,
Traffic police meeting their quotas,
The hour-long waits for the 101 bus,

The arrival of the 103 bus with three 101 buses behind it,
Two hour journeys to go across town,
30-minutes passing within a five mile radius,
The hills in the Heights,
The unisex salons on every block,
The hustle and the struggle,
The prices at Eli's and Citarellas,
The $.99 specials at Mc Donald's,
The billboards of Diddy and Jay
Promoting spirits and clothes in P.J's,
Fast cash and bad spending,
No education, no investments,
Flags of pride and lost souls,
False lifestyles, foolish acts,
Temporary trends,
Trying to fit in.
A woman with her mighty metrocard,
And her three kids all a year apart,
Fatherless babies, runaway girls depart,
The streets are unclean, crack fiends
In and out of reality.
Rush hour with noisy teens,
The homeless along with everyone else, crowded.
Pushing and shoving to get on the 6.
Walking passed the mural with Che,
Now ruined with graffiti
Up the steps into my warm apartment.
A key that works to get inside
Regardless of all the distress,

And constant stress, I realize that,
I'm blessed.

Last Words

I don't remember the last words that came out of her mouth, but I do recall her facial expressions. Her eyes were dilated, glossy, and her eyebrows were raised high. Her lower lip bent forward. She had not seen me in years. When I leaned toward her, I kissed her forehead and held her hand. She smiled. That must have been much more powerful then whatever her last words were. And now I don't feel so bad.

Witchcraft in the Pews *(Dedicated to "Pastor Cash" - Pass the cash and the prosperity gospel)*

There is witchcraft in the pews,
And sheep abused,
The doctrine is confused?
(Get the word of G-d)
Expose the false prophets,
A spiritual war,
But in the hands of G-d, I leave it all.

Wolves in Fleece *(The Experience at 12 Tribes)*

It was amazing to see these men worship the L-rd,
With their tassels, Star of David and pretty prayer shawls,
They were dressed like space men,
They were all dark and all from all nations.
But something in my heart felt something was wrong.
Smells like manipulation.

They spoke legit, like real sheep for the L-rd,
But my spiritual eyes saw something else,
The dark fog that I had ignored.

I walked into their temple and covered my head with a red kufi. The women sat on the right and men on the left, with no disputing.
I obeyed, but air was so thick,
Like dark fog and smog, yet I pretended it did not exist.

The women were silent.
The numerous babies cried.
No worship, no song, no dance.
The long lessons were dry.

Nine-hour readings,
With one-hour food breaks.
Brethrens were so serious,
Hugs were cold and fake.
I could not speak because of my gender.
And during bible study my hand was raised for participation, but no recognition.
I slid my fiancé a piece of paper with all of the bible answers, I respected the submission.

Posters of tribes related to non- white nations,
Dark nations were accepted but the whites were rejected?
But my atheist friend was seeking Yeshua,
I could not invite him? My faith was being tested.

What Yeshua did they worship?
Now smiles seem to show fangs,
And handshakes showed claws.
I rubbed my eyes, but things got worse,
I saw long shackles and shadows on the walls.

Teachings of the history of slavery could be redeemed,
By hate that was so extreme to heal low self-esteem.
In paradise the white man will not serve me.
Your doctrine is all wrong. Now all eyes on me.

Get your hands away from my neck.
Why are you calling me a pig?
This isn't the house of the L-rd,
I have to get out of this pit.
L-rd you were so right,
Many will come to deceive,
I thank you because you opened my eyes,
From those wolves in fleece.

Innocent Sheep, Listen Again!
(The Experience at DWC)

A proud look and a lying tongue,
And a hand that sheds innocent blood,
From innocent sheep and the innocent young,

Once sons of G-d but now a son of a man,
Being brainwashed about false hopes and plans.
Doing blasphemies in factories disguised as sanctuaries.
Know them by their fruits. What do they consume?
Real sheep know HIS voice but the goats are confused.

Prophets for a Profit

Profits for a profit, con artists who hustle, manipulate for fast money, so a church they create. Prophets for a profit, study the stars and our hands, but their revelations aren't from the L-rd, they are guided by the one below. Prophets for a profit are really psychics and pimps. A real prophet follows the L-rd and his profit is salvation.

Playing G-d

Animals are being cloned from adult DNA,
Mammals no longer made through a sperm and an egg,
Sex with robots with humanistic appearances,
Projects are being subject to fulfill a lewd experience,
Injections and illusions, like a fountain of youth,
Infections and viruses from manmade experiments,
Uncouth.

Cautious

On ice without skis,
In sand sinking quick,
Thoughts of unease,
Vision clouded and thick,
On a road split in between
Avoiding a trick,
A red light on my forehead,
Someone is ready to squeeze,
Cautious,
I remain cautious,
In a realm where flesh and bone have no place.

Death for $20 but Eternal Life is Free

Hello to you too.
What is this flyer for?
You say I am a positive person?
I have an inner light?
Why do you squint?
Why are you holding my hand?
Where are you taking me?
Why is this place so foggy?
Do you want to play cards with me?
I'm pretty good Black Jack.
Hey, my cousin wears shells in her hair.
Why all the crosses?
Why all the idols?
Are you a Christian?
Are you just spiritual?

You want me to place my money inside your bible?
Can I see which chapter it is?
Oh it's Isaiah I see.
Have you read this scripture before?
You say you can tell me my future?
Okay, I'll give you a 20.
I'll make it $50...
But only if you allow me to read
Isaiah 8:19.
I know you came here to tell me my future,
But I came here to tell you yours.
You see a long time ago,
I was in your seat,
And someone also gave me this word to read.
And now nothing is the same.
And that "inner light" you see,
Is not my aura or chi,
It is the Ruach HaKodesh,
The Holy Spirit in me.
So, you make a living in stacks of 20's,
But eternal living is free!
And when those 20's run out,
Where do you think you will be?

Red

Whether his eyes are like
The sunset, a starry night or blue sky,
Rounded or slanted like almonds.

Whether his skin is like the rich soil,
Sun kissed or milky and porcelain,

Smooth like silk or gritty like sand.

Whether his hair is like straw or curly like wool,

I'm certain his blood was red.

B.L.O.O.D.
Because **L**ove **O**vercame **O**ver **D**eath.

F.R.O.G.S.

You see green skin
and bulging eyes
upon a lily pad,
well look closer.
Fully **R**elying **O**n **G-d**'s **S**alvation (Yeshua).

Immanuel

There was a women being blessed,
a husband put to a test,
a life about to come but different from the rest.

They were visited by angels with messages in dreams,
They had to believe, soon the virgin would conceive.
This was the king that was once predicted,
the one from the scriptures

soon to grow up to be convicted
and slayed.

Immanuel is his name,
the future was about to change,
He will live on earth,
die in it,
and in heaven He will reign.

As He grew,
He walked in the villages with sandals,
preaching the word of the G-d,
causing scandals,
but he can handle...(this)

He's a teacher and a prophet,
but called a liar,
a madman,
had the life no one desired.

Had the power cure the sick,
heal the blind,
cast demons, and
turn water to wine.

A Nazarene, a king,

Salvation to the all the Jews?

(A woman yelled)
But where are his fancy clothes,

and where are his jewels?
Where's His crown?
Where's His robe?
And where is His throne?
This man is not a king,
He looks like he doesn't have a home.

Rejected by his people,
Betrayed by friends,
but those who loved him
knew his time was coming to an end....
yet begin.
He was sent to a trial,
sentenced to crucifixion for saying He was G-d's child.

He had to carry a cross,
while being pierced with spears,
the soldiers gambled his clothes,
his hands and feet were pierced.

He was beaten so bad
but had no broken bones,
He was given a sour drink,
the solders sold his clothes.

Hours passed by and Immanuel died.
His people mourned and cried.
But three days passed and to their surprise,
He rose and returned from the grave.

He paid in full,
all of the debt of sins,
grace and mercy were given
and a new life to begin.

Scarlet the Harlot's Last Day

She was happy,
Tonight was the last night,
The last customer,
The last cheap rubber,
No more infections and no more fights.

The last time being used,
The last time being abused,
No more lust, no more booze.

Another day another dollar,
She needed another motto,
Freedom was more valuable to her.
Away from this life was like hitting the lotto.

She thought about her new life,
Away from this grime,
Away from the fast money,
Drugs and crime.

Her pimp then showed up with another customer.
She began to frown.

He pulls her aside and said
"Scarlet, don't make me look like a clown!
I promised you that today,
Would be your last day,
But this money will be so great.
You won't regret it, don't dismay.

"What's the rush?
Did you find a real crush?
Who would want you?
Your lifestyle is like crap that I flush.

"Are seeking a soul,
To fill that empty hole,
You might find something to fill that void,
But what about those holes in those pretty arms you destroyed?

"I'm just kidding. You know I play rough.
Now here's a tissue, cut it out.
You got to be tough.

"Now go out there and make me proud,
There is a bonus in it for you if three is a crowd."

She wiped her tears and fixed her face,
Another crazy night she has to erase.
But she remained hopeful, and prayed for another day,
That it may be her last so she may run away, forever!

It's Time to Tell That Dude Goodbye

There was once a girl named Sue,
And her last name Icidal,
Always popping Prozac, prescription pills and Midols.
Her idols,
Were the ones in the tombs.
She never went outside,
Always stuck in her room.
Dark with fog,
Full of fumes,
Surrounded by bottles of glue,
Crack and heroine,
Her face pale blue.
Broken ropes on the chandelier,
Broken glass on the floor,
Empty bottles of beer,
Music blasting by Korn.
I looked inside her window,
She looked at me, she wept and said,
"I'm tired of living, I want to be dead."
I prayed, and she told me to go away.
I showed her my bible, and I asked if I could stay.
She came outside with big dark shades,
The sun bothered her.
I took her to place where I knew they would comfort
her.
She went inside, willing and fell on her knees,

Vomited, yelled, and started to seize,
The people prayed and started to intercede,
She began to weep and then tried to speak,
Because she knew that The L-rd is what she had needed,
To no longer be weak.

The enemy was once walking by your side,
The enemy was holding you tight,
Walking down the aisle, becoming his wife,
And all you did was cry, cry, and cry.
It's time to tell that dude goodbye,
It's time to tell that dude goodbye,
Because your true King has arrived
He is Adoni.

And All This Pain

(2x)And all this pain,
And all this pain is just to call out HIS name,
I know my purpose but my flesh gets too weak,
Sometimes it's so hard to get down on my knees,
Help me please!

The Master's Honey

A storm began to draw near, and the moon was out. The screeching of tires near the front gate signaled to the cat her Master had arrived. A light breeze from a cracked window blew the wick of a candle. The cat jumped and hid under her pink and white blanket that was placed underneath the kitchen table. She began to shiver on the cold wooden floor. She heard her Master's footsteps coming up the stairs. He slowly opened the door, dragging his big black muddy boots on his beige carpet. His house was dark. He had brown velvet curtains that always remained closed. He closed the kitchen window, and took out a match from the cabinet to light his favorite cherry scented candle. The Master took out his empty prescription medication from the cabinet which had been empty for about a month. He put the bottle back and slammed the cabinet door. He then served the cat some milk and tuna in separate bowls, and placed both underneath the table. The Master went into the living room and sat on his rocking chair. He rocked back and forth, waiting to see if Honey responded. She peeked from underneath her blanket. He narrowed his eyes until they were barely open. Honey leaned toward the bowl and the Master jumped on top of her. He sat Honey on his lap and stroked her head gently, gliding his fingers through her fur. She struggled to get off but he tightened his thighs, secured and pushed her against his lap. He then rocked back and forth as she slowly sank between his legs, until he fell asleep. She could not move. She had no strength and sat still between his heavy, sweaty legs. She had no other choice but to fall sleep. Sleeping is where Honey escaped her reality.

Honey walked toward the back of a diner that had bright neon lights. A man noticed her as he took out the trash and she approached him. He placed a mirror on the floor. She looked into the mirror. She saw her round dark pupils stretch before her, like a cat. She looked at herself confused and saw her black fishnet stockings, white tank, a red striped skirt and red high heels. She scratched her head and the lights went out.

The next day as the Master left for work, Honey climbed on top of the window ledge to watch him leave. She sat at the window for hours at a time. She stared at all sorts of cats: black, white, brown, olive, yellow and red, walking around freely. She was once a beautiful cat, but now sad and blue. Honey always stared at the cats outside her window but none ever looked back. This time a white cat stared up at her. Her windows were tinted. She thought the cat must have been looking at something else. But the white cat stared and stared.

That evening, she lay on her blanket waiting for her Master to arrive. Impatient and hungry, she sneaked into a cabinet and pulled out a bag of peanuts. She ate. She then heard the screeching tires from her Master's car, she ran underneath her blanket. He walked in with grocery bags in his hands. As he placed her bowl of milk on the floor he fixed his eyes on the trail of crumbs by the cabinet.

"Inpatient, are we?! Couldn't wait for me?!" He yelled as he kicked the bowl of milk on the floor.

Honey shivered uncontrollably and ran toward the rocking chair in the living room.

"Don't make me run, Honey. You won't get far; you know you'll just choke!"

She knew she had made him mad and the shackle she had on around her neck gave her limited mobility. She ran to the kitchen and hid under the blanket instead. He pulled her out from her blanket by her head and made her lick the milk off the floor. He smashed Honey's face against the floor, bruising her left cheek. She fought back and bit him on his hand. He lifted his arm into the air and made a fist. Honey went to sleep immediately. She started to dream.

Honey awoke in a dark alley, as the sound of wicked laughter echoed and pulled away in a green car. She was surrounded by cardboard boxes and trash. She tried to figure out her location, but she was lost. As she dusted herself off she saw a small diner across the street, and she limped toward it as a trail of maroon spots followed behind her. She went toward the back of the diner and saw a man throwing out trash. The man spotted her and he spoke,

"Hey there, are you okay?"

Honey peeked inside the open door and saw a kitchen. He went inside and came back out with a plate of leftovers. Honey ate. He then took off his black jacket and wrapped it around her shoulders. She noticed the blue engraved initial "M "on the jacket. She looked up at him. He was tall, with dark hair and a fair complexion. He had bright emerald eyes and a dark goatee that was neatly trimmed. All of a sudden a bright light shone behind them.

"Don't look back," said the man.

But Honey looked. The light was warm and welcoming. She walked toward it and wept. She cried for help. The man then walked toward her and blocked the light and said sinisterly, "I am your help."

While Honey was asleep, her Master picked her up and took her into his bedroom. She awoke to the sound of a zipper. Honey opened her eyes and fought him off. She tried to run toward the front door but couldn't. She scratched his left eye. The Master became so upset, he placed duct taped on her mouth and then taped her arms and legs together. He shoved her into the bathroom and closed the door. He then went into his room. Honey wept. She was tired of living. She wanted to die. Her only escape was in her dreams. She tried to close her eyes and dream. But she was not tired. Her reality was a nightmare. Honey stared underneath the crack of the door where the light of the moon reflected against the window. The moon was her only comfort in her dark world.

Hours passed.

Honey is sitting in a booth, inside a diner. A man approaches her. "Aren't you a pretty kitty," whispered the man.

"Excuse me?" said Honey. She surprised herself and held her mouth. It was the first time Honey had spoken. She noticed his jacket. It had a capital "M" engraved on the left side of his chest.

"I'm sorry, that was rude," said the man as he grinned.

Honey grew nervous and ran toward the exit. The man caught up to her and gave her a napkin dispenser. Honey took it and saw her image. Honey saw her round hazel colored eyed and long auburn hair. She tried to remove her smudged eye liner with her fingers and fix her smudged crimson lipstick.

"You see, you are a sweet puss."

"Do not call me that."

"Really? Why not?"

"Cats were a sign of royalty in ancient Egypt." The man's voice became a distant babble as Honey became distracted by the voices and laughter outside. She saw a green car circling around the block.

"Right," he said.

"What? I wasn't paying attention," said Honey.

"Of course not sweet heart, the only thing you care about is what's between your legs and the money you can get from it."

"Leave me alone," said Honey

"You are not a good kitty. You're not a sign of royalty. You are a bad kitty. And bad kittens are treated the same way they treat themselves, with no respect," said the man.

He punched her in her face. Honey fell to the floor. She wept and turned to her side. The alley was completely dark except for a bright light far away. Honey stared at the light as it flickered.

"Wake up Honey, get up," said the Master. Honey awoke as her Master carried her into a tub. "You need a bath," said the Master laughing.

He removed her duct tape. Patches of fur remained on the tape as Honey bled. She limped into the tub. Then the doorbell rang. The Master went to the door.

"I'll be back, Honey."

Honey limped toward the window and saw her Master drive off. She then saw the white cat at her window. The white cat jumped up and climbed to her windowsill.

Honey jumped on the windowsill as well. The white cat began to knock on the window. Honey couldn't open the window. She just stared into his fiery brown eyes. She wanted to feel the freedom he had, but Honey's shackle never allowed her to leave home. She became frustrated and went under her blanket. The white cat remained by the window. Honey then began to hear scratches on her door. Honey peeked from under the blanket. Her Master had arrived home. She noticed him struggling to come inside. Honey walked closer to get a better look. He was surrounded by many cats. The Master shook them off his legs and kicked them off the stairs. Honey drew near the living room. Honey obeyed and remained still. The cats continued to crawl on the Master. They climbed up his legs and jumped on his arms and shoulders. Honey tried to approach the door but knew she would not get passed it because of the shackle. Honey had never gone passed the rocking chair in the living room. But she continued to walk as far as she could. The Master yelled at Honey and warned her to stay put. Honey stopped, obeyed for fear of her Master. She lay down on the floor watching the cats fight her Master. More and more cats came. Some cats got into the home. Honey's emotions raced. She was scared, happy, and confused. She stared at the white cat. A black cat pushed her back legs. Honey knew they wanted her to escape but she could not. The cats stopped fighting. They all began to leave except the white cat.

"Where did all these cats come from?" said the Master.

The Master shooed the white cat out the door but it did not move. Honey walked toward the cat, but stopped when her Master yelled. Honey ran and hid underneath her blanket in the kitchen. The white cat ran out the door.

"Good girl, you obeyed." said the Master as he closed the door. "Those strays are crazy." He bent down and stroked her fur.

"Good girl, that's why you're my favorite puss."

Honey's eyes became watery. Her Master went into the bathroom to apply alcohol on his wounds. Honey looked at the door and glanced at her Master. Honey walked toward the living room and stared at the door. She thought about all the endless possibilities, the freedom, the bright light that she saw in her dreams.

She continued to walk to see how far she could go. She had never tested the length of the long shackle. Honey was not scared and she continued to walk. She reached the front door in amazement. Honey looked back to see her shackle, but it was gone. She blinked and blinked. There was no sign of a hole in the wall, there was no shackle present. She saw her home differently. The bedroom and kitchen looked far and the rocking chair did, too. She touched the door. Her Master saw her.

"Honey, where are you going? Remember that the, uh, shackle will choke you," he said nervously and confused.

Honey already knew there was no shackle and realized there never was. It was all in her mind. The Master moved slowly toward her. She was surprised to see he was no longer aggressive. She hissed at him and took out her claws, and noticed her claws were nails. She looked at her paws, but there were hands. She looked at him. She took a look at herself crawling on the ground and realized she had legs.

"Honey?" said the Master

Honey's legs and palms were fragile and wounded from crawling on her hands and knees. She got up and held on to the brown velvet curtains, but her weight dragged the curtain down. Lights came into the room. Her eyes burned.

Honey took down all the other curtains in the house and allowed the light to shine in. Although her eyes were weak she loved the sunlight. She saw her home. It looked like a dirty pit.

Honey opened the door.

The Master spoke. "Where are you going? This is your home. "

Honey opened the door. She smiled as the sun shone on her face. The brown, olive, black, red, and yellow cats she once saw on her windowsill now looked like beautiful women strolling with shopping bags, strollers, free. She noticed the white cat across the street. The cat was no longer a cat either, but a man wearing white. Honey held herself on the rail and walked down the stairs as best she could. The man in white watched from afar. The pedestrians watched her struggle. Honey had a bad stench. She wore a dirty tank top, black fishnet stocking and one heelless shoe. Her hair was knotted and filthy. Her face was swollen and bruised. The man in white approached her and placed his white blazer over her waste and tied it securely. He then smiled and walked away into a light. Honey tried to catch up but she tripped on her heelless shoe. A couple of pedestrians helped her up. The Master walked toward his door. Honey and the Master looked at each other from afar, eye to eye. She had realized that her life was all a lie and that her dreams were real. The shackles were an illusion. Her life was an illusion. Her dreams were reality and they told her about the past life, the one she had forgotten from the constant beatings. The Master knew Honey had finally awoken. He could no longer lie to her. He had lost Honey.

"You can no longer have me. I don't belong to you anymore," yelled Honey.

Although the Master was upset he began to smile at her.

The pedestrians' watched Honey yell. They saw no one by the door of the house. Honey watched the Master as he slowly walked back into the house. He disappeared into the darkness. All was pitch black with only the sight of white haughty eyes and the grin of sharp teeth.

The Good, the Bad, the Ugly, and Everything In Between

As my pen injects this pad,
I begin to think about my past,
I doodle, scribble, and draw,
Thoughts about all the things that I saw,
Clocks and sunsets, the seasons pass,
The friends that stayed and the ones that did not last,
The blurry visions caused by the shot glasses,

The sleepless nights, the nightmares that harassed,
The love I experience that was unconditional,
The freedom to sing and dance, inspirational,
The forgiveness, forgetting, repenting, and repeating
The realistic side of the human being,
Constant battling and constant retreating,
The lessons learned and the beatings,
The truth and the invention,
The comprehension and the tension,
Learning when to ignore and when to pay attention.
Prevention and protection,
Lukewarm and stale,
But growing, trying to prevail,
With the good comes the bad,
And everything in between,
To make you who you are,
A living testimony.

The Battle of the New Creature

I have to get right,
Or I am going to end up feeling the flames,
Conviction is being placed against my chest, stomach
and brain. I can't go on making final decisions,
While the L-rd just sits on his throne and just listens?
I know that I am only human, and I am assuming
That the feelings of confusion I should not be
consuming.

But I am growing, undergoing and I don't know much,
My identity and its shell are getting crushed.

Crucifixion of the Flesh

Crucifixion of the flesh is what's best,
I know it's a test,
That's why you always see me so stressed,
I can't get rest.
There is a battle inside.
A war in between,
But the spirit must decide, no comprise.
I cannot hide,
Because the L-rd sees my fruits,
And when something is growing spoiled,
Then you cut it from the root,
With no dispute, and no fighting,
And if that's the case,
Then you will easily give up and go back to your old ways.
(If you do)
Then you will be celebrating,
The shackles back on,
While the devil is getting happy inviting seven along,
And the chains are being placed, are so heavy and strong,
When the spirit is getting weak, then the devil is strong,
When the spirit is getting weak, then the flesh is strong.

When the spirit is getting weak, then The L-rd's reception is gone.
Celebrating the shackles back on,
That the spirit becomes so weak that the spirit is gone.

What's Going on in My Mind? *(Spooky Lyrics)*

Seeing images, crazy thoughts in my mind,
False illusions, I'm getting scared,
What's going on in my life?
No TV and no reading,
But I still can't believe what I'm seeing,
Lack of eating, lack of sleep, man, this is deep.

I feel like I'm getting drunk in my mind,
Having fatal thoughts of suicide, not wanting to cry,
In and out my bed,
Hearing voices in my head,
I can't go to sleep,
Because I know something is coming ahead.

The lights better come on,
There's something going on,
I know I'm losing it but,
What did I do wrong?
As I pray I see that things get worse,
Maybe it's just a family curse,
Should I just sit and watch,
Or maybe things will get even worse.

Then I pray a little harder,
Hold open my armor,
Read a little, see if things get calmer.

As I walk around,
I walk straight into a mirror,
Reflection is gone,
I feel a presence coming nearer,
It's a reflection of a demon making faces at me,
I jump a run away and now it's laughing at me.

I pause for a minute and wonder if that's how I look,
Or does that live inside of me?
Oh man, now I am shook.
I'm just a little kid playing it cool,
I go home to ask for help
But they think I'm playing the fool,
I tried to explain, let them know that this isn't a game,
They call me sick and they call me insane,
They try to get me to a doctor but I am feeling fine,
I'm just worried about the things going on in my mind.

My family's remedy is to keep me occupied,
They put me to sweep, do chores, but I can't touch knives,
Season to season and years pass by,
The voices come and go and there is nowhere to hide,
They tell me; sooner or later we will meet again,
And this will continue until we are friends, amen,
NOT!

This is not G-d,
I know this is wrong,
But how long will this go on, the presence is strong,
Feeling used and abused, confused and wronged,
Feeling raped, not in a physical but mental state.
The years passed by, the feelings have arrived,
All I do is cry, all I do is weep.
Feeling something grabbing my feet and touch my cheek, I pray for the L-rd for my soul to keep.
My life is disrupted, I feel so corrupted,
My mind has erupted, and it's about to explode,
Can't handle it anymore,
All these things being exposed,
My childhood wasn't right since I was nine years old,
And when I lay down I see darkness and fog,
Floating green eyes without a face,
And movable dolls,
Bed springs move down,
Someone's on my bed,
I'm being pressed down,
I can't move my head,
I'm punching it and kicking it off,
The energy is gone,
I got to turn the night light on, (Thank G-d)
Another night, another fight,
Just clearing my head,
I kiss my rosary and then I go to bed,
My leg feels a stroking, my rosary has me chocking,
How longer will this go on?
I start to rebuke,

Light comes into my room,
Now I see angels in the corners of my room
With their swords and spears,
Telling me I have nothing to fear,
Call on his name,
Salvation is near.

Lost Ones

Some have...

Lost themselves to hand signs and violence,
Others to bullets by their own hands,
Some are lost in cells and four white walls, others are
Those taught to seek advice in candles and crystal balls.

Others lost in pills, needles and bottles,
Noses stuffed and spent on destitute illusions of reality,
Endless days of bowing down to idols and statues,
Sinking deep into vanity, spurges and debt.

Salvation to the Nations

Blow the trumpet in Zion,
For here comes the Lion,
He is the Lamb that was slay,
He is the truth and the way,
The key to eternal light and salvation,

Spread the word to all the nations.

Define Divine

Like fine wine,
Refined,
We are the branches,
He is the vine,
From the beginning of time,
Of creation and design,
The way, the truth and the life combined,
He is Defined Divine.

Poems, Prose, Phrases and Phases

The Poems are my thoughts on paper,
Prose are the stories of situations,
And phrases from the book of salvation guided me through my Phases in life.

*******************Thank You*********************

First and foremost, this book of poems, lyrics, stories and testimonies, is dedicated to the King of all Kings, my L-rd and Savior, Yeshua. To my family and friends who supported me. I thank you for your encouraging words. I thank you for the love. To my step-daughter Tiffany, you are something special, we look alike, have bad memories, and we love books, although I did not birth you, you are my daughter. My sisters Diana, Jannine, and Tania. My uncle Thomas for giving me my first tape recorder. My aunts Dasia and Daisy for being there when I was down and always keeping me on my toes. To my cousins Messy Yesi, Alej, and Angel for the creative, funny videos and music we made together To the thousands of other cousins as well. To Reb Benzi and Erika for your prayers and support as well to all the members of Kehilath HaDerekh, the congregation of the way. To the CCNY professors, for all those advanced poetry and creative writing classes I took. To Flip and his family, to Brother P aka Phil and his family. To Dale Norvell for his amazing picture, Exposition ©2010, found at deviantart.com, to whom I give full credit for the cover of *Poems, Prose and Phases*. To those who were a part of my childhood, adolescence, and adulthood, whether friend or foe, those who lasted and to those who did not, you were part of my journey. To the talented Raquel Penzo for taking time to read and edit my work. Thanks for all you do. I appreciate you. To my mom and dad for my life. Dad, one day we will reunite again. Mom continue to be one of the strongest women I know, you are amazing. Last but definitely not least, my best friend, my love, my number one fan and supporter, my husband, Roy. I thank The L-rd, Most High, G-d in Yeshua, for blessing me. Thanks again.

www.ingramcontent.com/pod-product-compliance
Ingram Content Group UK Ltd.
Pitfield, Milton Keynes, MK11 3LW, UK
UKHW040557210726
13854UKWH00008B/1384